MICK MANNING and **BRITA GRANSTRÖM** have won
many awards for their picture information books, including
the Smarties Silver Award and the English Association Award.
In 2013, their huge contribution to children's literature was recognised
with a nomination for the prestigious Astrid Lindgren Memorial Award,
the largest international children's and young adult literature award in the world.
Their books for Frances Lincoln include *The Beatles, Charles Dickens:
Scenes from an Extraordinary Life, What Mr Darwin Saw, Tail-End Charlie,
Taff in the WAAF, The Secrets of Stonehenge, Dino-Dinners, Woolly Mammoth,*
the *Fly on the Wall series: Roman Fort, Viking Longship, Pharaoh's Egypt*
and *Greek Hero, Nature Adventures* and *Wild Adventures.* They have four sons,
and divide their time between the North of England and Brita's
homeland of Sweden. Find out more about their books at
www.mickandbrita.com.

For Gemma-saurus and Vera-saurus

The Authors and Publishers would like
to thank Dr Angela Milner, Deputy Keeper of Paleontology
at the Natural History Museum, London for her help and advice.

Dino-Dinners copyright © Frances Lincoln Limited 2009
Text and Illustrations copyright © Mick Manning and Brita Granström 2009

First published in Great Britain in 2006 by Frances Lincoln Children's Books,
74–77 White Lion Street, London N1 9PF
www.franceslincoln.com

This paperback edition published in Great Britain and the USA in 2015

A catalogue record for this book is available from the British Library.

ISBN 978-1-84780-665-9

Illustrated with watercolour and pencil

Set in Base Twelve and The Sans

Printed in China

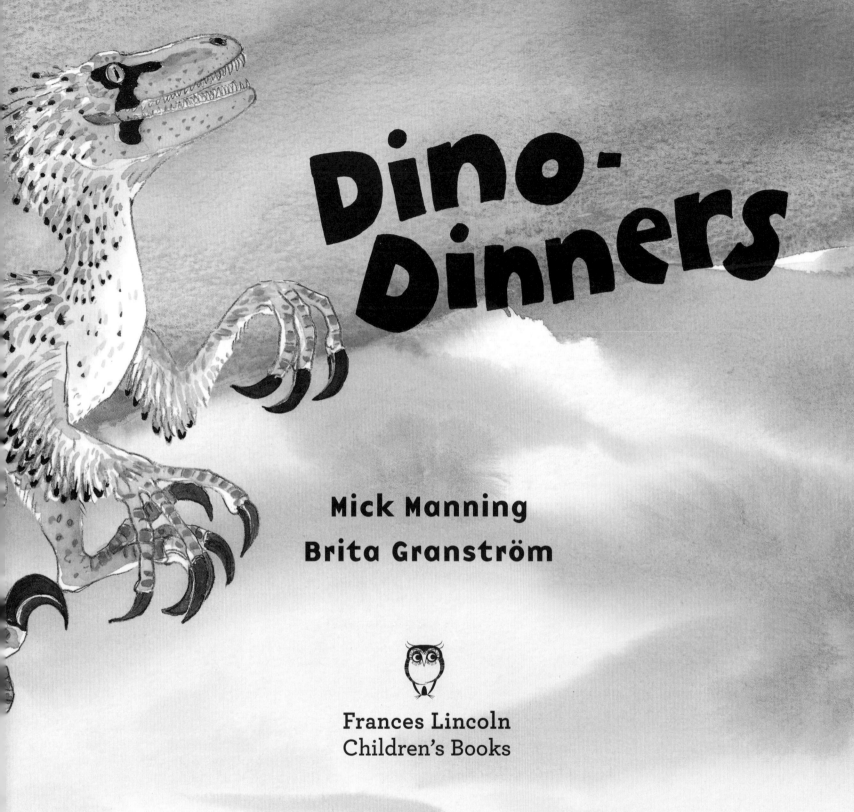

Dino-Dinners

Mick Manning

Brita Granström

Frances Lincoln
Children's Books

In association with the
Natural History Museum, London

Oviraptor

I eat cones, shellfish and nuts –

cracking eggs can be tasty too.

Best of all, a fat crunchy beetle,

snatched from the top

of a dinosaur poo.

Oviraptor

(Oh-vee-rap-tor)
* Lived 85 – 75 million years ago
* Nose to tail: 1.8 metres
* Omnivore

Oviraptor stood on two legs and was a fast emu-sized dinosaur.

Nobody is sure what *Oviraptor* ate but it was probably omnivorous, eating both plants and meat.

Using its strong beak, it could easily have crushed nuts, bones, insects, eggs and shellfish.

Euoplocephalus

(You-op-loh-keff-ah-lus)

* Lived 74 – 71 million years ago
* Nose to tail: up to 7 metres
* Herbivore

Euoplocephalus' heavy clubbed tail could inflict broken bones on predators. No predator wants to risk that. A serious injury means 'game over'.

Euoplocephalus' tail weighed up to 30 kilos. Its tailbones were strengthened to swing this heavy weight.

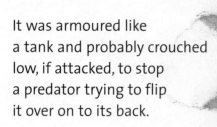

It was armoured like a tank and probably crouched low, if attacked, to stop a predator trying to flip it over on to its back.

H ere I come!

Trundling through the woodland plants,

I'm always on the look-out

for danger as I munch.

Armoured legs, armoured body, armoured face,
clubbed tail a-swinging – just in case.

Mind out!

Tyrannosaurus rex

(Tie-ran-oh-sore-us rex)

* Lived 67–65 million years ago
* Nose to tail: 12 metres
* Carnivore

Tyrannosaurus rex's crushing bite and keen sense of smell meant that it could feed on the largest herbivores – alive or dead!

Tyrannosaurus nestlings would have been covered in downy fluff to keep them warm.

Tyrannosaurus rex

I like sick and injured dinos,

or dead dinos that really pong!

I'm a giant with a giant's appetite

and I love rotten meat –

it doesn't put up a fight!

Triceratops

(Try-ker-ah-tops)
* Lived 67–65 million years ago
* Nose to tail: 9 metres
* Herbivore

Teeth-marks that match *Tyrannosaurus rex* teeth have been found in the fossil bones of *Triceratops*.

Triceratops would have charged like a modern rhino.

Triceratops

I eat plants – but be warned!

I'll charge anyone, anytime!

My horns have six tons of muscle

and bone behind them.

I am a very dangerous veggie.

You'll soon see,

if you ever mess with me!

Edmontosaurus

I am one of a crowd – a herd that trumpets and grunts
to each other. My jaws and cheeks help my teeth grind,
grate and crush: turning every delicious mouthful
of my veggie dino-dinner into mush.

Edmontosaurus

(Ed-mont-oh-sore-us)
* Lived 76– 67 million years ago
* Nose to tail: up to 13 metres
* Herbivore

Edmontosaurus was a hadrosaur living in herds in open plains and woodlands.

Its jaws moved in a unique sideways chewing movement making its teeth act like a cheese grater.

Some hadrosaurs had bony crests to recognise others of their own kind. Some called to each other using large 'trumpet' chambers in their heads.

Velociraptor

(Vel-oss-ee-rap-tor)

* Lived 86 – 73 million years ago
* Nose to tail: 1.8 metres
* Carnivore

Velociraptor was a pack hunter like modern wolves.

Velociraptor had feathers to keep warm. Flapping feathered arms may also have helped it balance.

A *Velociraptor* and a *Protoceratops* were found fossilized together! They died fighting each other and were covered with blowing sand.

Huge toe claws helped it climb up on to the backs of large prey.

Velociraptor

Big or small, there's no escape
once my gang give chase.
We sprint… and leap,

climbing leathery mountains of dino flesh
with the huge claws on our feet.

Then comes our favourite part –

EAT! EAT! EAT!

Coelophysis

(Seel-oh-fie-sis)

* Lived 225 – 220 million years ago
* Nose to tail: 3 metres
* Carnivore

Coelophysis lived early in the age of dinosaurs.

Fossilised *Coelophysis* have been found with chewed-up young in their stomachs.

They may well have been under stress from starvation and drought, but this still makes them dino-cannibals.

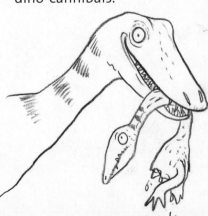

Coelophysis

We prowl the landscape, hunting for prey.

When times get hard we'll eat

our own kind if they get in our way.

Iguanodon

Pond plants are a tasty dino-dinner for us.
We browse slowly and quietly,
munching as we move.
Then comes the noisy part –

the more we eat,
the more we fart!

Iguanodon

(Ig-wha-noh-don)
* Lived 130 – 115 million years ago
* Nose to tail: up to 10 metres
* Herbivore

Iguanodon used
the 'little finger' on each
hand to grip and pull
leafy stems to its mouth.

All that plant food
made *Iguanodon's*
large stomach fizz up
like a bottle of pop,
producing a lot of gas!

Iguanodon's huge thumb
spike was its only defence
against predators like
Baryonyx.

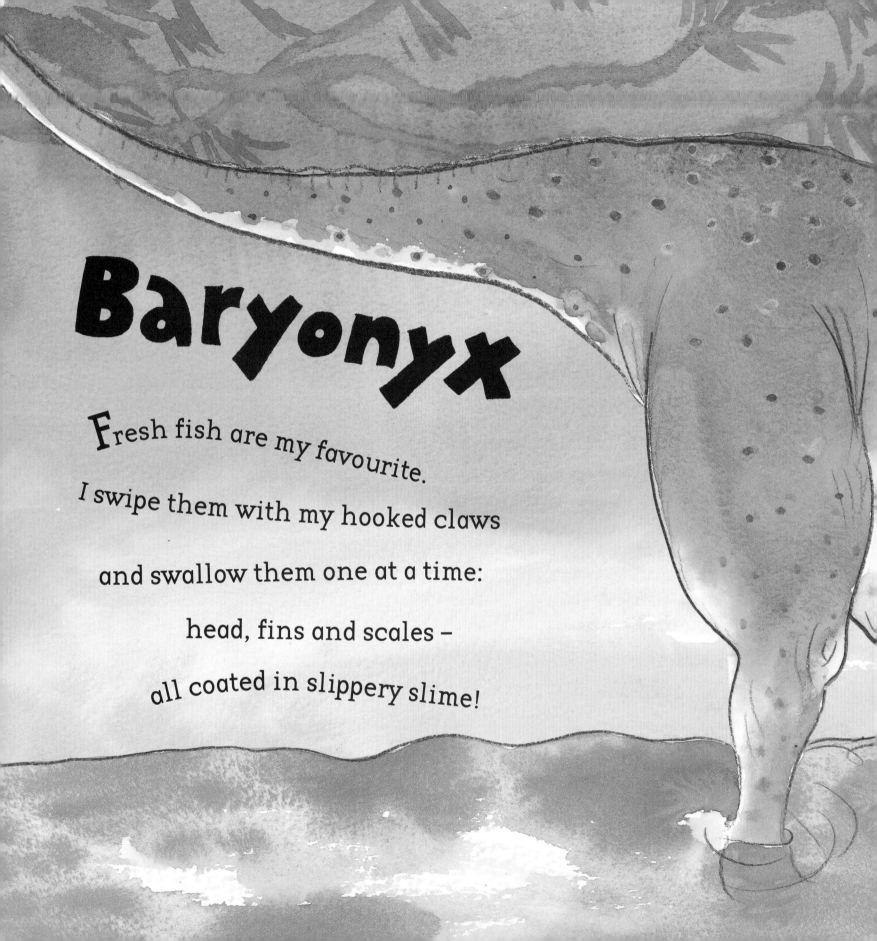

Baryonyx

Fresh fish are my favourite.

I swipe them with my hooked claws

and swallow them one at a time:

head, fins and scales –

all coated in slippery slime!

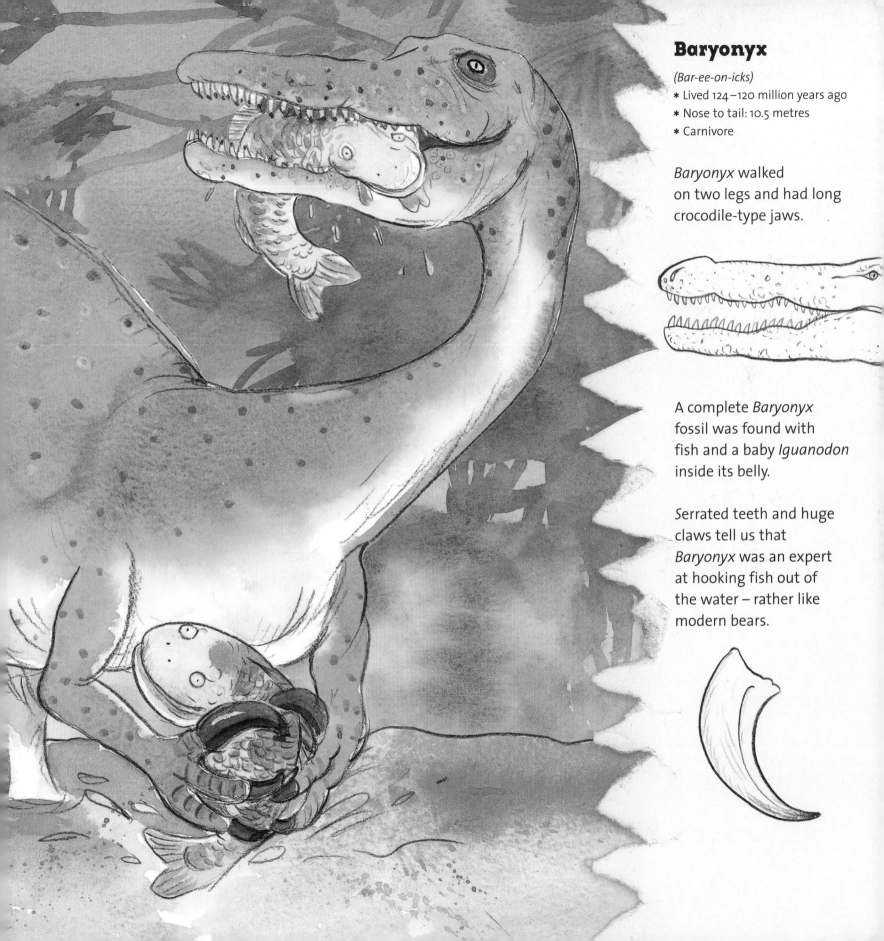

Baryonyx

(Bar-ee-on-icks)
* Lived 124–120 million years ago
* Nose to tail: 10.5 metres
* Carnivore

Baryonyx walked on two legs and had long crocodile-type jaws.

A complete *Baryonyx* fossil was found with fish and a baby *Iguanodon* inside its belly.

Serrated teeth and huge claws tell us that *Baryonyx* was an expert at hooking fish out of the water – rather like modern bears.

Brachiosaurus

(Brak-ee-oh-sore-us)

* Lived 155 – 140 million years ago
* Nose to tail: up to 25 metres
* Herbivore

Brachiosaurus and some other plant-eaters swallowed small pebbles called gastroliths to help digest the plants they ate.

Brachiosaurus didn't chew but raked food into its mouth with peg-like teeth.

Brachiosaurus

With our long necks

we can nibble treetop salad.

It tastes green and fresh with
a tangy flavour of pine nuts.

We rake and swallow.

We don't bother to chew.

But treetop salad always makes us…

POO!

The huge amount of plant material *Brachiosaurus* ate meant that it made enormous poos – rather like giant elephant droppings.

Fossil poos are called coprolites and they tell dinosaur experts a lot about what dinosaurs ate.

Glossary

Cannibal
An animal that eats other animals of its own kind.

Carnivore
An animal that eats only meat.

Coprolites
Fossilised poo that can tell us a lot about what different dinosaurs had for dinner.

Drought
When it doesn't rain for a long time, plants and animals die because they can't find anything to drink or eat.

Fossil
The remains of animals and plants that have been dead and buried for so long that they turn to stone.

Gastroliths
Some plant-eating dinosaurs swallowed pebbles to help them break up the tough plant fibres in their stomachs.

mya = million years ago

248 mya   Triassic   **205 mya**   Jurassic

Hadrosaur
The name given to the family of 'duck-billed', plant-eating dinosaurs to which *Edmontosaurus* belonged.

Herbivore
An animal that eats only plants.

Omnivore
An animal that eats both plants and meat.

Predator
An animal that hunts other animals for food.

Prey
An animal that is hunted by other animals for food.

Scales
Small, hard plates that cover fish, reptiles and other animals.

Serrated teeth
Teeth with notches or grooves on their edges that make a good cutting surface, like a knife.

Starvation
When there isn't enough food to eat, animals are so hungry that they start to die.

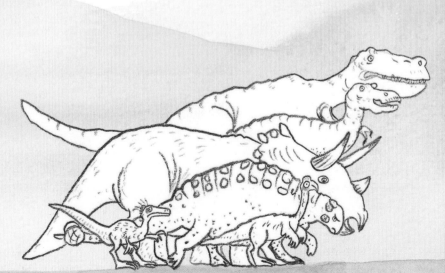

Cretaceous

Woolly Mammoth

What were woolly mammoths really like? How did they survive in the Ice-Age cold? And why were they hunted by our human ancestors? Go back in time to the world of these extraordinary animals and learn all about the lives of mammoths, from feeding, grazing and fighting to their family bonds.

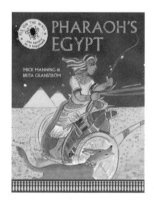

Fly on the Wall: Pharaoh's Egypt

Be a fly on the wall in the time of the ancient Egyptians. See how the mummy-makers perform their grisly work, sail down the Nile with Huya the scribe, and creep into the tombs with robbers as they steal jewels by torchlight. Packed full of up-to-date information about the world of the Pharaohs from the latest archaeological discoveries, this book shows you ancient Egypt as it really happened!

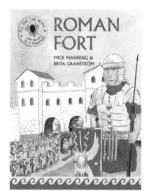

Fly on the Wall: Roman Fort

Be a fly on the wall in the time of the Romans. Patrol with a windswept centurion, eavesdrop on Roman nobles in the smelly toilets and dine at a tasty banquet. Packed full of up-to-date information about the world of the Romans from the latest archaeological discoveries, this book shows you Roman history as it really happened!